How to Catch a Roadrunner

3
Simple
Principles
That Can
Transform
Your Life

How to Catch a Roadrunner

3
SIMPLE
PRINCIPLES
THAT CAN
TRANSFORM
YOUR LIFE

Neil A. Rock
and John S. Sproviero

How to Catch a Roadrunner
3 Simple Principles That Can Transform Your Life

Neil A. Rock
and John S. Sproviero

Copyright © 2004
Neil A. Rock and John S. Sproviero

Published by:
Red Tail Publishing
Wake Forest, NC 27587

Printed in the United States of America

ISBN: 0-9763850-1-5

CONTENTS

FOREWORD

Having been introduced to the VWV concept through the tale of Max and the roadrunner, it is now time for you to apply the same principles in your own life. The prerequisites are few and simple: Having a dream and allowing yourself a few minutes each day. There are no age, gender, ethnic, or financial requirements involved.

The value of having goals has been well documented. They add a purpose and meaning to our lives, helping us to focus on whatever it is *we* deem to be important. Setting goals and ultimately achieving them does not have to be a time-consuming, often-intimidating procedure. As the roadrunner noted, regarding the VWV concept: "Its foundations lie in logic and are surpassed only by its inherent simplicity."

You will now be introduced to many noteworthy individuals who have used all or some portion of the concept to accomplish their personal goals—people like Albert Einstein, Suze Orman, Tiger Woods, and Jim Carrey, to name just a few. Hopefully, these examples will inspire and encourage you to take a similar approach. After all, there is no patent on success and happiness.

Next, you will have the opportunity to begin applying the VWV concept to your own life. The section on categories will help you to see the many areas where goal setting can be of benefit, followed by the time frames that will help you to stay focused on their resolution. Finally, you are provided with the means to immediately begin writing down *your* goals—however large or small they may be.

May you come to experience the same peace and prosperity enjoyed by Max, Tom, the rabbit, and all the other creatures in the land. Both Neil and I wish you happiness and success in all future endeavors.

John S. Sproviero
Westlake, Ohio
December 2003

PREFACE

There are two things I know for certain about myself: I love to dream, and I believe in keeping things simple.

I dream by using my imagination to create a vision of what could be. In grade school I was like most other kids, dreaming of throwing the winning pass in the Super Bowl or winning gold medals in the Olympics.

"Keeping things simple" has been a consistent theme throughout my life. It was hard for me to understand why so many people tended to complicate matters for no apparent reason. I agree with Albert Einstein who once said, "Everything should be made as simple as possible, but not simpler." To me, taking something that is seemingly difficult, seeing through the clutter, and simplifying it to what really matters can save a lot of time and effort.

As I grew older, I noticed that many of my dreams were indeed coming true…and that using a simple concept was helping me to make it possible. First, I visualized what I wanted. Next, I wrote it down on paper. Then I kept it in a prominent place where it would always remain visible.

During the past few years, I've spoken to thousands around the country, sharing how this simple concept can help them realize *their* dreams and goals. Many have written or called to say how successful this method has been for them and their families, with accomplishments such as...

- Writing a novel
- Running a marathon
- Learning to speak Spanish
- Competing in the Paralympics in Spain
- Remodeling a kitchen
- Buying a second home on the beach

Because of this, I came to realize another truth about myself: I enjoy helping people, especially when it involves achieving their dreams and goals. This insight became the impetus for the book.

If you've made it through this preface, the most difficult part is over. The rest is simple, fun, and very effective! As an unrelenting optimist, I firmly believe that you can accomplish anything you set your mind to. If you want more out of your life, stay true to the concept outlined within this book and begin to realize *your* hopes and dreams.

If you forget everything else, just remember one thing: **VWV!**

Neil A. Rock
October 2004

Introduction

"Three weeks from now I will be harvesting my crops; imagine where you will be and it will be so."

Taken from the movie *Gladiator*, this is how Maximus (Russell Crowe) addressed a small group of Roman soldiers minutes before a battle. To better prepare them for combat, he was encouraging his men to visualize a goal—to think about where they would like to be and what they would like to be doing three weeks in the future. Maximus was helping his soldiers to focus, to be relentless in pursuit of their visual goal. An interesting concept. The warriors would fight harder and more skillfully because they had a clear vision of where they would be in three weeks…and what they would need to do to get there. When the subconscious mind first embraces a vision, the actions necessary to realize it will follow.

Planning our own lives is no different. Where would you like to be and what would you like to be doing in three weeks? One year? Five years?

To fulfill your dreams, they must be woven into the fabric of your life. Success rarely occurs spontaneously. Accomplishing goals—converting dreams

13

into reality—requires a game plan. The plan of action outlined in this book begins and ends with a simple yet effective model: VWV (Visualize, Write, Visible). First, *visualize* your dreams and goals, *write* them down, and then keep them *visible* to you.

Using the VWV concept *in its entirety* will allow for the best opportunity to achieve anything and everything, just as the roadrunner did because Max was quite skilled as a hunter. At times, it may be appropriate to use only a portion of VWV, but by incorporating the entire model, you enhance the likelihood that goal attainment becomes a reality. VWV is easy and fun to use, so simple that anyone old enough to read and write can benefit from it. You only need to have a dream.

We have already heard from many people whose lives were enhanced by the model—men, women, and children—all desiring some improvement in a wide array of categories. From simple things like finally getting around to changing that burned-out light bulb or saving money for a new car...to one forward thinker who desired to become an astronaut and fly to the moon!

Don't be afraid to catch the roadrunner in your life. May all of your dreams come true.

How to Catch a Roadrunner

1

VISUALIZE

Visualization can be a simple, enjoyable process. All it takes is an imagination and a little time (it doesn't require a pyramid-shaped stone to stand on, but it might help!). To visualize goals, simply think about where you would like to be or what you would like to accomplish. *Really* think about it, as if you were playing a movie in your head. Here is an intriguing example:

Major James Nesmith was an average golfer, with scores usually in the mid-to-high 90s. He dedicated little time and effort towards improving his game. It wasn't until Major Nesmith became a prisoner of war in North Vietnam that he began to play golf again. He was placed in solitary confinement—in a four and a half by five-foot cage—alone, with no activity or anyone to speak with. Here, the Major began to play golf in his mind. It helped pass the time…and keep him sane.

He used all five senses to create the most realistic golf round possible, on a course he had played many times before at home. Major Nesmith could feel the wind, smell the freshly cut grass, and hear the sound of birds in the trees. The attention to detail with which he approached these visualizations was impressive. Nesmith recreated every step, placing his golf bag down, choosing a club, taking practice swings, seeing blades of grass flying up off the ground…you get the idea. In addition, all aspects of a perfect swing were visualized: He would feel the contact with the ball, then watch it soar on line towards his target. Major Nesmith played the course four hours a day, seven days a week, for seven years…in his mind.

Fortunately, Major Nesmith was released from captivity. After seven years as a POW, out of shape and in poor physical condition, Nesmith played the actual course that he had played so often in his mind.

Nesmith shot a 74, twenty strokes lower than his best score ever.

Many war prisoners have used visualization to stay alive and preserve their sanity when forced with overwhelming circumstances. Imagine the success you could have in the comfort of your own home.

In 1964, Colonel Floyd Thompson's plane was shot down over Vietnam, and he wound up being the longest-held POW in American history. After nine years in captivity, abused both mentally and physically, Colonel Thompson was asked how he managed to survive such an ordeal. Believe it or not, he survived by *building a house*! For nine years, he used his mind to visualize the construction of a home that he and his wife could live in. Colonel Thompson lived because he had a goal—a goal that he visualized every day. Albert Einstein, the world-renowned physicist known for his brilliant mind, once said, "Your imagination is the preview to life's coming attractions." Major Nesmith and Colonel Thompson are "living proof."

What would you like to accomplish? Visualize yourself accomplishing your goals, and they will soon be reality. Let's say your goal is to run in the Boston Marathon. Imagine in great detail everything about race day. You're in great shape due to the many days and months of training leading up to the event.

"If you can dream it, you can do it."

Walt Disney

Next you see hundreds of people—an elite group of athletes—lined up to run the marathon along with you. You have trained many hours, and are now prepared to run a race that very few people would ever attempt.

Close your eyes, take a deep breath, and smell the cool morning air. Hear the roar of the crowd as the starting gunshot sounds, feel the other racers close in as you fight for space, actually taste the water from the paper cups offered to you as you pass through the first five miles. You are doing it. You set a goal to run in the Boston Marathon, and mentally you are there.

There are two major benefits provided by visualization. First, by using the mind to practice, you are preparing yourself mentally to succeed. Also, because you have rehearsed the event or accomplishment so many times, comfort and ease replaces the usual stress. The task will no longer seem foreign or intimidating to you.

Actor Arnold Schwarzenegger once said, "What I am most happy about is that I can zero in on a vision of where I want to be in the future. I can see it so clearly in front of me when I daydream that it's almost reality. Then I get this easy feeling, and I don't have to be uptight because I already feel like I'm there, that it's just a matter of time."

The mind is a powerful tool—harnessing the visualization concept can make any event seem real. A goal is attained because you've already accomplished it many times in your mind.

The key to visualization is *practice*, using the technique on a daily basis. Whether it's during a workout, in the shower, before you go to bed, or after you first wake up in the morning, surround yourself with thoughts of successful completion and the goal will be accomplished far sooner than you ever could have imagined.

Athletes commonly use visualization to improve performance. The pre-shot routine for many golfers is to visualize the ball headed towards the target. Football running backs visualize the hole forming in front of them, dodging tackles as they head towards the end zone. In a 1998 *New York Times* interview, baseball home run-hitter Mark McGwire said he used the visualization technique. When asked how he managed to hit seventy home runs in one season, McGwire replied, "I visualized my bat making contact with the ball."

Political figures, charged with the responsibility of heading nations, must have a vision of the future in order to lead. In 1961, President John F. Kennedy gave a speech to congress and said, "I believe that this nation should commit itself to achieving the goal *before the decade is out*, of landing a man on the moon and returning him safely to earth." On July 16, 1969, Apollo 11 lifted off from *Kennedy* Space Center. Four days later, astronaut Neil Armstrong uttered the immortal words, "That's one small step for man, one giant leap for mankind," as he descended upon the moon's surface.

Business executives often attribute the technique to their success. A *Wall Street Journal* article mentioned visualization as one of six common activities employed by these leaders. They would rehearse future business meetings mentally in preparation for the actual event. "Top chief executives imagined every facet and feeling of what would have to happen to make a presentation a success, practicing a kind of purposeful daydreaming." We all daydream. Daydreaming with a purpose will help you to achieve goals.

Visualization is not limited to personal, sports, or business goal attainment. It has even been taught to patients as a prescription for healing their illnesses.

**"The mind always
tries to complete
what it pictures."**

Dr. Norman Vincent Peale

How to Catch a Roadrunner

When the world-famous bicycle racer Lance Armstrong was diagnosed with testicular cancer, he used the power of his mind to fend off the disease, even after it had metastasized in his lungs and brain. He refused to accept the 3 percent chance of survival given to him by physicians.

In his book, *It's Not About the Bike*, Armstrong claimed that his success in beating cancer was due in part to his strong mind. He visualized the HCG blood counts (the bad ones) in his body lowering over time. "I began to set goals with my blood, and I would get psyched up when I met them...I would concentrate on that number, as if I could make the counts by mentally willing it."

Lance Armstrong has been cancer-free for over eight years. In that time, he has won six of the most physically taxing competitions in all of sports— The Tour De France—and he did it in successive years.

Finally, visualization is currently being taught as a vehicle to accomplish perfection, albeit on the golf course. The Swedish duo of Kjell Enlager and Pia Nielson espouse a concept known as *Vision 54* as part of the training for professional and elite

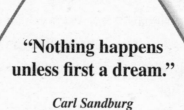

"Nothing happens
unless first a dream."

Carl Sandburg

How to Catch a Roadrunner

amateur golfers from their country. It appears to be working. In 2002, one out of eight of the LPGA tour's leading money winners hailed from Sweden, a country with 1/32 the population of the United States.

A form of *negative* visualization hinders many golfers. "With *Vision 54* we talk about things that are impossible today and how to make them possible tomorrow," says Nielson. On a typical par 72 golf course, *Vision 54* involves hitting every fairway, every green in regulation and one putt per hole. That's 18 straight birdies, resulting in the unthinkable score of 54. Enlager and Nielson believe that most golfers have birdied every hole at their home course at least one time—just never during the same round. Unthinkable? Maybe, but consider this:

On all professional tours, 59 has been the lowest score posted in a sanctioned event, the feat being accomplished by five different male golfers. During the second round of *The Standard Register Ping* tournament in March of 2001, a female golfer began her day with 8 consecutive birdies. Her round ended with a total of 13—just 5 shy of the perfect 54—making her the first female golfer ever to break the 60 barrier.

Annika Sorenstam is a Swedish golf professional who utilizes *Vision 54*. At age 34, she has won 56 tournaments and was recently inducted into the LPGA Hall of Fame. "It's very important," Sorenstam says of her goal setting. "And why is it important? Because that motivates me, and that pushes me. If I can visualize something, then it is easier for me to work there...I need to see things. Goals are things I can understand, I can touch."

In 2002, Annika won 13 events—more than half of those she entered. Many golf writers commented on her fabulous year by comparing her to Tiger Woods, the male golfer and most famous athlete in the world. "Tiger may be a better player," they said, "but Annika had a better year." Many career goals remain for Annika, including the strong desire to be remembered as the best female golfer that ever lived—a goal her male counterpart Tiger shares. I wouldn't bet against her.

"The vision that you glorify in your mind, the ideal that you enthrone in your heart. This you will build your life by, this you will become" proclaimed writer James Allen. Visualize *your* dreams and aspirations...and watch them become reality!

2

WRITE

"Gain a clear vision of your dream and then define it in writing," says author Steven Scott. You will not completely commit yourself unless your dreams and goals are *written*.

As you begin to visualize and write your goals, you might start to notice that you are in the minority; only 3 percent will actually take the time to do so. It's worth your time to be a part of this minority.

Ever hear of Anthony Robbins? In *Awaken the Giant Within*, this well-known motivational speaker tells the story of a train trip he once took to Russia. Says Robbins, "With nothing to write on but the back of an old Russian map, I wrote down all my

"The tools and
strategies I've used
to create a life I love are...
First, I invest time and money
on my personal development.
Second, I periodically create
a visual map of my desires.
Third, I commit my goals to paper."

Cheryl Richardson, CEO & Founder of Life Makeovers

How to Catch a Roadrunner

long-term goals…on that day, I set specific goals that transformed my life." Years later, when asked to explain how he made such incredible shifts in his life, Robbins produced the Russian map that contained his goals. "It was amazing to see how many I'd achieved," he said. The back of that old Russian map gave Robbins the *direction* he needed to achieve his goals. Whether it's on a bridge, in the sand, or on a tree (remember the roadrunner?) *just write them down*.

To further demonstrate, Mark McCormack, founder of the International Management Group, once said, "Write it down anywhere—on a Filofax, a legal pad, a scrap of paper, or the palm of your hand—but *get it down in writing*. Writing it down is the first step in any action. It articulates your desire to do something. It is a reminder when you get swamped. It eliminates the excuse that you forgot."

McCormack continued, "But most important, writing it down is a commitment—a signed contract that gives you the momentum to achieve your immediate goals." Writing a goal will help you ingrain it into your daily routine, making it as simple as eating, sleeping, or breathing. Even with the best intention, a spoken goal can easily dissipate.

Did you know that…

John Gruden's written goal while in college was to be the head football coach at the University of Michigan by the age of 39. At 39 he was head coach of the Superbowl Champion Tampa Bay Buccaneers!

How to Catch a Roadrunner

"It's a dream until it is written, then it's a goal," said Emmitt Smith's high school football coach. Before each NFL season, Smith writes down his football goals for the year. Smith's accomplishments speak volumes. In 2002, Smith became the NFL's all-time leading rusher, surpassing Walter Payton.

Children, as well as adults, can benefit from written goals. The book *Chicken Soup for the Soul* tells the story of Monty Roberts, a grade school student who wrote a paper about his future goal to own a horse ranch. With careful attention to detail, Roberts drew a diagram of his 200-acre dream, including a detailed floor plan for a 4,000-square-foot house that would sit on the property. His teacher told him to rewrite the paper and be more realistic about his goal or receive a failing grade. Roberts didn't rewrite his assignment. As a matter of fact, Roberts still has that original paper framed over the fireplace of his 4,000-square-foot house in the middle of his 200-acre horse ranch. Roberts used a written goal as motivation and commitment to achieve his dreams.

Physician and writer Oliver Wendell Holmes once said, "The great thing in this world is not so much where we are but in what direction we are moving." Regardless of past events or present circumstances,

"I am young,
powerful, and successful,
producing at least
$10,000 a month."

Suze Orman's written goals

How to Catch a Roadrunner

written goals can provide a new direction for your future. Consider the journey of Scott Adams, a middle manager at Pacific Bell, who clung tightly to his childhood dream of becoming a syndicated cartoonist. After working seventeen years for the company, he decided to make a career change. Adams began by writing the goal "I will become a syndicated cartoonist" fifteen times each day. Today, Scott Adam's popular comic strip *Dilbert* can be read in newspapers across the country.

A similar story involves a waitress in California who was making only $400 a month. Following an unfortunate experience with an investment firm, she decided to make the business her career. After securing a broker's position at Merrill Lynch, the former waitress began writing down her goals. "I am young, powerful, and successful, producing at least $10,000 a month" was what she recorded each day on a piece of paper.

Suze Orman succeeded in the investment business with Merrill Lynch and subsequently built her own successful investment company. "I created what I wanted for myself first on paper. Every morning before I went to work, I would write it over and over again," she recalls. Today, Orman has assembled a

"Writing something down is the first step towards making something happen."

Lee Iacocca

multimillion-dollar enterprise consisting of a book publishing program, a syndicated radio show that is televised weekly, a column in *O* magazine, two PBS pledge shows, and a Web site that attracts more than eight million readers each month. Orman had a vision of a successful career, and a written goal helped her to realize the dream.

Do you remember the percentage of people who actually write down their goals? This final example will hopefully persuade you to become one of them.

In 1953, one hundred graduating seniors from Yale University were involved in an interesting study. They were asked questions about their career aspirations, *and* if they had written down all of these future desires. The study revealed that only three of the one hundred seniors of the 1953 Yale graduating class had written goals.

Twenty years later, the one hundred study participants were polled again. This time the questions focused on personal success, accomplishments, net worth, etc. Remarkably—or not so, depending on how you look at it—the three seniors with written goals in 1953 had a greater net worth than the other ninety-seven students combined!

First *visualize* the goal, and then steer your dreams in the right direction by *writing* them down. "Put down on paper what you want to accomplish," writes author David Schwartz. It's that simple.

3

VISIBLE

"Unstoppable achievers keep their eyes on the target at all times," writes author Cynthia Keasey. "They often use visual keys to remind them through the day of the goal they're working toward."

The VWV formula is not complete without the last V, which stands for *Visible*. Once you've visualized a goal and written it down, keeping it visible is the final piece in the process. Putting it on display *visibly* plays a vital role in ultimately achieving the goal, yet it's an often-overlooked component. Imagine making a detailed grocery list and not bringing it with you to the store; the effort you put into writing the list has been wasted. As the roadrunner noted,

> "What good is it
> to write down a goal
> and then stick it in a
> drawer somewhere,
> or bury it in the sand?"
>
> *The Roadrunner*

How to Catch a Roadrunner

"What good is it to write down a goal and then stick it in a drawer somewhere, or bury it in the sand." It needs to be displayed prominently as a reminder of what you desire to accomplish.

Keeping a written goal *visible* makes it come alive—it breathes life into your goal. Displaying your goal visibly also eliminates the need for complicated action steps, processes, and procedures involving your written goal. In essence, it makes recording a goal simple. There is no right or wrong way to do it. To write, "I want to be president of the company" or "I need to spend more time with my daughter" is sufficient as long as you *visibly* display it.

The most recognized sports figure in the world uses a visible reminder to stay focused on his professional goal. By simply taping a large number "18" to his office wall, Tiger Woods reminds himself to work towards being the greatest player *ever* in his sport. The number of major championships a player has accumulated over his career defines true greatness in golf. Most agree that with 18 major wins, Jack Nicklaus is arguably the greatest ever, but Tiger may have something to say about it before all is said and done. By age 28, Woods has already won eight majors and still has plenty of time left.

"Shane pinned the card
to the wall next to his bed...
so that it was the first thing he
would see every morning,
and the last thing he would
see at night."

Sports Illustrated on Shane Battier

How to Catch a Roadrunner

Wood's example demonstrates that any form of a visible goal can be effective. A number can serve as a visible goal, as could a picture or object. By wallpapering his home with the likeness of Max, the roadrunner was constantly reminded of his goal. Whatever you decide to use, just keep it visible.

Although it's common for athletes to be goal setters, little is spoken of accomplishments made outside of their profession. Shane Battier is a NBA basketball player who applies visible goals to personal development and achievement. An article in *Sports Illustrated* describes Battier: "At the age of 12 he was the number one chair out of 106 trumpets in Birmingham's annual youth orchestra concert. After earning a near perfect score on the entrance exam, he entered Detroit Country Day School in the seventh grade... As an 11th grader Shane delivered the commencement speech to the graduating seniors at *another* area high school. He conducted part of his interview with Duke admissions director Christoph Guttentag in German. The Blue Devils' associate athletic director, Chris Kennedy, recalls returning home after his first encounter with Battier, in 1996, and when his wife asked him about his day, he responded, 'I just met a kid who's going to be president someday.'"

"Keeping a written
goal *visible* makes it
come alive—it breathes
life into your goal."

It's obvious that Battier is an intelligent man and recognizes the genius of simplicity: Battier has been keeping his written goals visible for years. The article in *Sports Illustrated* notes, "At the stroke of midnight on Jan. 1, 1993, Shane Battier, then 14, began writing on an index card 10 goals he wanted to accomplish in the next year. Shane pinned the card to the wall next to his bed in his family's house in Birmingham, Mich., so that it was the first thing he would see every morning and the last thing he would see at night. His goals ranged from building a giant city out of Legos, to saving a human life. He also aspired to start as a ninth grader on the varsity at Detroit Country Day School. When he was named to the starting five the following fall, he went home, stared at the card and said, "Wow, this really works!"

Battier is an intelligent, worldly individual that lets nothing get in the way of what he desires to achieve.

This final example demonstrates the value of being creative in how you choose to display a visible goal. Authors Mark Victor Hansen and Jack Canfield were looking for "a million dollar title" for their new book. Ultimately, the title *Chicken Soup for the Soul* surfaced.

Jeff Davidson writes, "Mark took a copy of the New York Times best-seller list, and using the same font and point size, pasted '*Chicken Soup for the Soul*, by Mark Hansen and Jack Canfield,' over the number-one position for nonfiction books. Mark then posted his 'best-seller' list on the wall so he could see it all the time, claiming that he drew 'dynamic energy' from it." The overwhelming success and popularity of their book has been well chronicled. Hansen and Canfield had a vision, a goal, and a *novel* approach in keeping it visible.

Now you've seen how effective and simple it is to keep your written goals *visible*. Whether your goals are posted on the wall, refrigerator, desk or the dashboard of your car, just put them where they will be seen throughout the day. You'll be surprised how quickly your dreams become reality. To help you get started, we have provided goal-setting pages at the end of this book.

CHAPTER

4

VWV

You've read several examples of people who have been successful using one, or perhaps two, of the VWV components. Just as the roadrunner needed to use all of VWV to accomplish his goal, imagine how successful you could be by doing the same. One last inspiring example utilizes the VWV formula the way it's intended to be used—in its entirety.

In 1995, Barbara Walters interviewed a young man who visualized his goal, wrote it down, and kept it visible.

After dropping out of high school, he took a job as a janitor in order to help support his struggling family. At one low point, the family was forced to

"'VWV' is my way
of completing any
task, large or small,
or accomplishing any
goal I set my mind to."

The Roadrunner

live in a van. When the young man was fifteen, he and his father wrote a comedy routine, which was later tested in a small Toronto club. The evening didn't go well. Although the routine was labeled as boring and generally ridiculed, the young man remained faithful to his dream.

With the full support of his family, the aspiring comedian moved to Los Angeles in the late '80s to perform his routine. Following each performance on the club circuit, he drove his car to a Hollywood mountaintop, raised his arms and began to visualize. Concentrating on imagery, he imagined personnel from the entertainment industry wanting to work with him, including discussions regarding his financial value.

Shortly thereafter, he wrote himself a $10 million check for "acting services rendered"—his financial goal to be attained by Thanksgiving 1995. He placed that written goal in his wallet, where it could be seen every time he reached in for what little money he had. He kept that check in his wallet for four years; it became a visible reminder of what he wanted to achieve. After visualizing his goals, writing them down, and keeping them visible, he soon began to realize his dreams.

As his value to the industry slowly became apparent, he won roles in *Ace Ventura*, earning $350,000; *Mask*, pulling in $450,000; and *Dumb and Dumber*, which drew a $7 million salary. The three movies grossed over $300 million dollars at the box office. Jim Carrey never gave up his dream of entertaining people and making them laugh.

In 1995, Jim Carrey's prophetic gesture took on a life of its own when he signed a $10 million contract to appear in a *Mask* sequel.

Unfortunately, Carrey's father passed away earlier that year. The comedian confided that he'd placed the check in his father's shirt pocket as a tribute and symbol of fulfilling a dream. Carrey said, "It was his dream too." Jim's father had also been a gifted comedian, but opted for a more secure job to support his family. Rather than pursue a career for himself, the elder Carrey encouraged his son's ambition.

Carrey used the entire VWV model and accomplished his incredible $10 million goal. Now it's your turn. Don't put this mission off—the longer you wait for the perfect moment, the less likely you will be to put pen to paper. Heed the advice of writer Henry James, who wrote, "It's time to start living the life you've imagined."

5

GOAL-SETTING CATEGORIES

Written goals should be organized and specific. Categories will help you to stay focused and have a clearer picture of everything that's important to you.

The following six categories can help you to start achieving goals in many areas of your life: Family, Personal, Financial, Career/School, Health & Fitness, and Spiritual. Choose any or all of these categories, and take the time to reflect on where you are today, what you have accomplished thus far, and what you would like to achieve in the future.

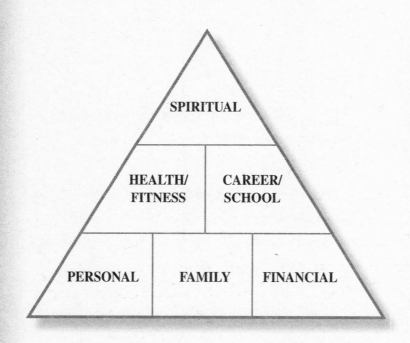

How to Catch a Roadrunner

Do you have family goals? Are there areas in your family life that you can improve?

What about your personal goals? Do you have any personal goals in your life that you have pushed aside or forgotten about as time has passed?

Could your financial situation be better? Do you have college funds for the children?

How's your career? Are you happy where you are working today? Have you thought about your next position and what it will take to get there?

Is your health where you want it to be? Are you living the lifestyle that will help you live longer and be healthier? Are you seeing your physician at least once a year for a physical?

Lastly, are you satisfied with your spiritual self? Do you spend time thinking and acting on your spiritual needs?

These are just some of the questions that you can think about as you begin to use goal-setting categories to plan your future. Just remember to keep them organized and specific, but more importantly, personal to your own goals and dreams.

6

GOAL-SETTING TIME FRAMES

"Forsake all inhibitions. Pursue thy dreams!" Walt Whitman said many years ago. Sometimes it's difficult to know when to set goals—in other words, what time frames are required for their completion. We've simplified this process with the time pyramid. There are four time categories in which most goals can be framed: Lifetime, Five-year, One-year, and Daily.

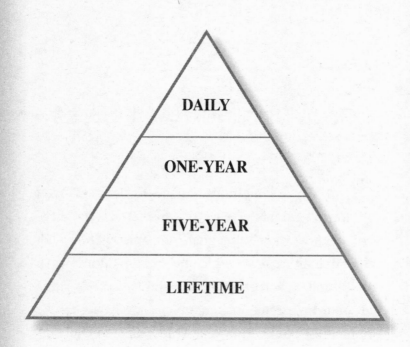

DAILY

ONE-YEAR

FIVE-YEAR

LIFETIME

LIFETIME GOALS

Notice that the bottom of the pyramid lists your lifetime goals. It is the foundation from which other goals can be built. Tommy Newberry, in *Success Is Not an Accident*, says, "If you don't have specific goals written down for your life, you are mentally malnourished. Your mind was designed to be fed with goals just as your body was designed to be fed with food and water." Your lifetime goals should be big and exciting. Pick a goal that you would like to be able to reflect upon someday and say, "I did it! I took chances...I seized the day!"

Arnold Schwarzenegger is a perfect example. In 1966, he was quoted as saying, "I want to be the greatest bodybuilder in the world, the greatest bodybuilder of all time, and the richest bodybuilder in the world. I want to live in the United States and own an apartment block and be a film star." Ironically, Arnold sold himself short when he visualized his lifetime goals. To this list of accomplishments, he could have added marrying into one of America's paramount political families and being elected governor of California.

The man *Readers Digest* calls "the real Indiana Jones," John Goddard, is another wonderful case in point of how to set lifetime goals. In 1939, when

Goddard was fifteen years old, he was at home one evening doing homework when he overheard a conversation of his elders. Reflecting back on their lives, they spoke with regret regarding many things they desired to accomplish, but never took the time to pursue. It was at this time that Goddard put his homework away and spent the next five hours writing a list of 127 challenging, lifetime goals that he wanted to accomplish. He wanted to make sure he didn't look back at his life with the same regret.

Here is a sample of what Goddard recorded that night:

- Explore eight of the world's major rivers, including the Nile, Amazon, and Congo
- Climb sixteen of the highest mountains including Everest, Kenya, and the Matterhorn
- Learn to fly a plane
- Circumnavigate the globe (he's done this four times)
- Visit the North and South Poles
- Read the Bible from cover to cover
- Play the flute and violin
- Study primitive cultures in twelve countries

The list goes on and on. At the age of sixty-one, Goddard had accomplished 108 of those original 127 goals.

When asked what caused him to create this fascinating list in the first place, he replied, "Two reasons. First, I was fed up with adults telling me what to do and what not to do with my life. Second, I didn't want to be fifty years old and realize I hadn't really accomplished anything."

Goddard lived an extraordinary life because he took the time to think about and write his lifetime goals. You also deserve to live an extraordinary life, so take time to think (visualize) what you want to accomplish in your lifetime. It took Max (with the aid of the roadrunner) years to discover his true purpose, but you can start now. And don't be afraid to think big. Use some of Goddard's goals as an example of how to approach this exercise. Then write them down on the pages provided at the end of this book.

FIVE-YEAR GOALS

Mark Victor Hansen once said, "By recording your dreams and goals on paper, you set in motion the process of becoming the person you most want to be."

Five years is not that far away, so take inventories of where you are today in respect to any or all of the six categories. Then begin to visualize your life in five years. What does it look like? More importantly, what do you want it to look like?

Think about your specific goals. Remember, what's important to one individual may not be to another. The same applies to a time frame—a one-year goal for you may be more realistic as a five-year goal for someone else. We also have to balance our goals, making sure our priorities are in line with them. A financial goal of traveling four days a week in order to get a new business started would conflict with a personal goal of coaching your son's soccer team.

With this in mind, begin to imagine what your life will look like in five years. What does your family life look like? What are your five-year family goals? Maybe you want to take your parents on a trip to Italy or host the first extended family reunion at your home.

What about your financial situation? Perhaps you desire to save $5,000 for each child's college fund or $20,000 for the beach house you've always dreamed of. Maybe graduating with an MBA in five years is a reasonable career goal or starting a consulting firm with ten clients under contract.

How to Catch a Roadrunner

Have you started looking for that sailboat that you've always wanted to buy and refinish...or started planning for that month-long bike tour of Europe that you've been thinking about?

What about your health and fitness goals? Have you started training for those three marathons that you want to complete in five years? Maybe you want to achieve the black belt level in martial arts.

Finally, what do you envision for your spiritual life in five years? Are you on the planning committee of your local church? Have you taken the time to investigate religions that might appeal to you?

Act fast! Five years will be here and gone before you know it.

In the space provided, write down some of your five-year goals. Think about the six categories we spoke of earlier, or of other areas in your life that you would like to plan for. Write as many goals as you wish. There is no magic number that works—the number is yours and yours alone. Also, notice there is not an in-depth, structured format that has sub-goals, objectives, and action plans. We believe that if you simply write down what you want to accomplish and keep it visible *daily*, you will then begin to work toward that goal without the need of a lengthy plan.

ONE-YEAR GOALS

Call it 1 year, 12 months, 52 weeks or 365 days—the point is, it will go by very fast. As you begin to fill in the one-year goal page, keep an important point in mind. Be very specific with your written goals. The more specific you write your goals, the higher the probability you will achieve them. After you think about a goal, always ask yourself, "Can I be more specific?" For example, perhaps you want to begin to exercise in the New Year. To some this is a goal, but writing, "I would like to exercise three days a week, lifting weights Monday, Wednesday, and Friday at 6:30 am" is more specific and appropriate.

Maybe you have a one-year family goal to coach your child's spring soccer team, or take the family on a week-long vacation to Disneyland the last week of August. One of your one-year financial goals might be to have all of your credit cards paid by December 31. Possibly you'll want to investigate college savings plans and start investing $50 a month by March 1.

A one-year personal goal might be to become a certified scuba diver, just in time for your honeymoon the week of July 8. Or perhaps you'd like to

How to Catch a Roadrunner

join a book club by September 1 and participate in monthly discussions.

Could this be the year you enhance your career? Maybe you'll enroll in a fall semester graduate program, or become one of the top 3 percent of your sales force by June 30.

Certainly, your one-year health and fitness goals will be important. Remembering to schedule your annual physical by March 15, or to begin exercising aerobically for twenty minutes every day might be appropriate. Think about your one-year spiritual goals. Perhaps you'll want to volunteer for two activities at your local church, or you may want to begin saying prayers at bedtime with your children.

These examples demonstrate the wide array of possible goals—they are not intended to suggest what's appropriate for your own personal situation. A lot can happen and change in one year, but you can lead the charge by *visualizing* what you want to accomplish, then *writing* it down, and keeping it *visible*.

Begin thinking about your one-year goals, then write down as many as you desire.

DAILY GOALS

Your most productive days will begin after taking a few minutes each evening to write down what you want to accomplish the next day. In doing this, you set into motion subconscious thoughts that help plan and ultimately achieve your goals. The next morning, this visible list can be carried with you, checking off each goal as it is accomplished. It's no different than preparing a list for the grocery store. You write down the items needed, and then check them off as you find them in the store. Your daily goals list can be handled the same way—just maintain the habit all year round.

Consider this example from Hyrum Smith's *The 10 Natural Laws of Successful Time and Life Management* about Charles Schwab, then president of Bethlehem Steel.

Schwab was struggling over some productivity issues and time constraints. Schwab challenged management consultant Ivy Lee, "Show me a way to get more things done with my time and I'll pay you any fee within reason."

Lee told him to write down on a piece of blank paper the most important jobs for the next day and

How to Catch a Roadrunner

then prioritize them by importance. He encouraged Schwab to mark them off as he achieved them and not to give up on *any* of the written tasks. Lee said you must "make this a habit every working day. When it works for you give the idea to your management. Try it as long as you like. Then send me your check for what you think it's worth.'"

A few weeks later, Schwab sent Lee a check for twenty-five thousand dollars, a lot of money in the 1930s. Schwab passed the idea on to his management team, claiming that the simple idea of writing down what he wanted to accomplish the next day was solely responsible for "turning Bethlehem Steel into the biggest independent steel producer in the world at the time." Schwab was quoted as saying, "Aren't all ideas basically simple?"

If this can turn Bethlehem Steel around, think what it can do for your life. Take five minutes in the evening to write down what you want to accomplish the next day. Finally, don't be afraid to make changes to your goals as time passes. For Max, his obsession regarding the chase was altered after his unique encounter with the roadrunner. Time tends to change our needs and wants in life, so we need to adjust our goals accordingly.

"Nothing happens unless first a dream," said American poet Carl Sandburg. Dreams—visions—are the foundation of all goals. Enhance your chances of attaining them by writing them down and keeping them visible. Have fun in the process, and always remember what *THE* roadrunner taught Max...VWV!

THE FOLLOWING ARE GOALS I WILL STRIVE TO ACCOMPLISH IN MY LIFETIME

X _____
signature

_____   _____

_____   _____

_____   _____

_____   _____

_____   _____

_____   _____

_____   _____

_____   _____

_____   _____

_____   _____

_____   _____

_____   _____

_____   _____

How to Catch a Roadrunner

I COMMIT TO ACHIEVING THE FOLLOWING FIVE-YEAR GOALS BY _____
month / day / year

X _____
signature

PERSONAL

_____

_____

_____

FAMILY

_____

_____

_____

CAREER/SCHOOL

_____

_____

_____

FINANCIAL

_____

_____

_____

HEALTH & FITNESS

_____

_____

_____

SPIRITUAL

_____

_____

_____

OTHER

_____

_____

OTHER

_____

_____

I COMMIT TO ACHIEVING THE FOLLOWING ONE-YEAR GOALS BY _____

month / day / year

X _____

signature

PERSONAL

_____

_____

_____

FAMILY

_____

_____

_____

CAREER/SCHOOL

_____

_____

_____

FINANCIAL

_____

_____

_____

HEALTH & FITNESS

_____

_____

_____

SPIRITUAL

_____

_____

_____

OTHER

_____

_____

OTHER

_____

_____

MY DAILY GOALS

Date: _____

✔ *achieved*

_____   _____

_____   _____

_____   _____

_____   _____

_____   _____

_____   _____

_____   _____

_____   _____

_____   _____

_____   _____

_____   _____

_____   _____

_____   _____

_____   _____

_____   _____

MY DAILY GOALS

Date: _____

✔ *achieved*

_____   _____

_____   _____

_____   _____

_____   _____

_____   _____

_____   _____

_____   _____

_____   _____

_____   _____

_____   _____

_____   _____

_____   _____

_____   _____

_____   _____

MY DAILY GOALS

Date: _____

✔ achieved

_____   _____

_____   _____

_____   _____

_____   _____

_____   _____

_____   _____

_____   _____

_____   _____

_____   _____

_____   _____

_____   _____

_____   _____

How to Catch a Roadrunner

MY DAILY GOALS

Date: _____

✔ achieved

_____   _____

_____   _____

_____   _____

_____   _____

_____   _____

_____   _____

_____   _____

_____   _____

_____   _____

_____   _____

_____   _____

_____   _____

_____   _____

_____   _____

_____   _____

How to Catch a Roadrunner

MY DAILY GOALS

Date: _____

✔ achieved

_____   _____

_____   _____

_____   _____

_____   _____

_____   _____

_____   _____

_____   _____

_____   _____

_____   _____

_____   _____

_____   _____

_____   _____

_____   _____

_____   _____

How to Catch a Roadrunner

My Daily Goals

Date: _____

✔ *achieved*

_____ _____

_____ _____

_____ _____

_____ _____

_____ _____

_____ _____

_____ _____

_____ _____

_____ _____

_____ _____

_____ _____

_____ _____

_____ _____

How to Catch a Roadrunner

My Daily Goals

Date: _____

✔ *achieved*

_____	_____
_____	_____
_____	_____
_____	_____
_____	_____
_____	_____
_____	_____
_____	_____
_____	_____
_____	_____
_____	_____
_____	_____
_____	_____
_____	_____

My Daily Goals

Date: _____

✔ *achieved*

_____   _____

_____   _____

_____   _____

_____   _____

_____   _____

_____   _____

_____   _____

_____   _____

_____   _____

_____   _____

_____   _____

_____   _____

_____   _____

_____   _____

How to Catch a Roadrunner

MY DAILY GOALS

Date: _____

✔ *achieved*

_____   _____

_____   _____

_____   _____

_____   _____

_____   _____

_____   _____

_____   _____

_____   _____

_____   _____

_____   _____

_____   _____

_____   _____

MY DAILY GOALS

Date: _____

✔ *achieved*

_____   _____

_____   _____

_____   _____

_____   _____

_____   _____

_____   _____

_____   _____

_____   _____

_____   _____

_____   _____

_____   _____

_____   _____

_____   _____

_____   _____

My Daily Goals

Date: _____

✔ *achieved*

_____   _____

_____   _____

_____   _____

_____   _____

_____   _____

_____   _____

_____   _____

_____   _____

_____   _____

_____   _____

_____   _____

_____   _____

_____   _____

_____   _____

_____   _____

How to Catch a Roadrunner

MY DAILY GOALS

Date: _____

✔ *achieved*

_____   _____

_____   _____

_____   _____

_____   _____

_____   _____

_____   _____

_____   _____

_____   _____

_____   _____

_____   _____

_____   _____

_____   _____

_____   _____

_____   _____

MY DAILY GOALS

Date: _____

✔ *achieved*

_____   _____

_____   _____

_____   _____

_____   _____

_____   _____

_____   _____

_____   _____

_____   _____

_____   _____

_____   _____

_____   _____

_____   _____

_____   _____

_____   _____

How to Catch a Roadrunner

MY DAILY GOALS

Date: _____

✔ achieved

_____   _____

_____   _____

_____   _____

_____   _____

_____   _____

_____   _____

_____   _____

_____   _____

_____   _____

_____   _____

_____   _____

_____   _____

_____   _____

_____   _____

How to Catch a Roadrunner

MY DAILY GOALS

Date: _____

✔ *achieved*

_____	_____
_____	_____
_____	_____
_____	_____
_____	_____
_____	_____
_____	_____
_____	_____
_____	_____
_____	_____
_____	_____
_____	_____
_____	_____
_____	_____
_____	_____

MY DAILY GOALS

Date: _____

✔ *achieved*

_____   _____

_____   _____

_____   _____

_____   _____

_____   _____

_____   _____

_____   _____

_____   _____

_____   _____

_____   _____

_____   _____

_____   _____

_____   _____

_____   _____

How to Catch a Roadrunner

MY DAILY GOALS

Date: _____

✔ *achieved*

_____ _____

_____ _____

_____ _____

_____ _____

_____ _____

_____ _____

_____ _____

_____ _____

_____ _____

_____ _____

_____ _____

_____ _____

_____ _____

_____ _____

How to Catch a Roadrunner

My Daily Goals

Date: _____

✔ *achieved*

_____   _____

_____   _____

_____   _____

_____   _____

_____   _____

_____   _____

_____   _____

_____   _____

_____   _____

_____   _____

_____   _____

_____   _____

MY DAILY GOALS

Date: _____

✔ *achieved*

_____   _____

_____   _____

_____   _____

_____   _____

_____   _____

_____   _____

_____   _____

_____   _____

_____   _____

_____   _____

_____   _____

_____   _____

_____   _____

_____   _____

How to Catch a Roadrunner

MY DAILY GOALS

Date: _____

✔ *achieved*

_____   _____

_____   _____

_____   _____

_____   _____

_____   _____

_____   _____

_____   _____

_____   _____

_____   _____

_____   _____

_____   _____

_____   _____

_____   _____

_____   _____

_____   _____

MY DAILY GOALS

Date: _____

✔ *achieved*

_____ _____

_____ _____

_____ _____

_____ _____

_____ _____

_____ _____

_____ _____

_____ _____

_____ _____

_____ _____

_____ _____

_____ _____

_____ _____

_____ _____

_____ _____

How to Catch a Roadrunner

MY DAILY GOALS

Date: _____

✔ *achieved*

_____   _____

_____   _____

_____   _____

_____   _____

_____   _____

_____   _____

_____   _____

_____   _____

_____   _____

_____   _____

_____   _____

_____   _____

_____   _____

_____   _____

How to Catch a Roadrunner

ACKNOWLEDGMENTS

Although I'm grateful to many people who have influenced me over the years, the following individuals warrant mention for the impact they made on this project.

First to my wife, Robyn, whose support and tolerance allowed me the time to pursue and research my passion. Your inspiration has helped me accomplish so many things. Thank you for everything you do.

To my grandfather Charles Tonkin, whose name lives on in my son Ryan Charles Rock. Etched in my memory are his written "lists" of things to do. I can still see him crossing them off as each one was accomplished. My grandfather taught me many things during those memorable times we spent together just sitting in his driveway talking. I could have listened to his stories forever.

To John Sproviero, whose writing gave us the vehicle to reach people all over the world. This collaborative effort is the epitome of teamwork, allowing each of our talents and true passions to surface.

And finally to my mother. None of this would be possible without your dedication to our family. Your commitment is uncompromising. You taught me how to persevere and accomplish goals in spite of adversity.

I would also like to thank Tim Koegel for his exceptional advice and constant inspiration and Al Redding for his support in getting our first manuscript off the ground. Also, to Norma Collins whose editing and professionalism is unmatched, and Barb and Jim Weems for bringing this all together for us and making the process fun. Finally, to Melody Morris for her support and expertise in the book business and Frances Tonkin for her keen eye.

ABOUT THE AUTHOR

Neil A. Rock has over 16 years of professional experience in the Pharmaceutical industry. He is currently the U.S. Sales Director of Leadership Development with *GlaxoSmithKline,* having earned the company's highest sales honor four consecutive years. Neil won NCAA All-American honors in Track & Field while attending Southeast Missouri State University. He graduated with a degree in Business Administration and later received his Masters from Kent State University. Driven by the art of goal setting at an early age, Neil searched for a simpler system—resulting in the VWV concept and the original Goals Journal in the year 2000. Neil has had the opportunity to give his unique goals presentation all over the United States. Neil resides in North Carolina with his wife Robyn and children Ryan, Reagan and Nolan.

For more information about
Neil A. Rock and John S. Sproviero
or to order books, go to:

www.CoyoteVision.com